A Kid's Guide to Drawing America™

How to Draw
Kansas's
Sights and Symbols

Jenny Deinard

The Rosen Publishing Group's
PowerKids Press™
New York

Published in 2002 by The Rosen Publishing Group, Inc.
29 East 21st Street, New York, NY 10010

First Edition

Book Design: Kim Sonsky
Layout Design: Michael Donnellan
Project Editors: Jannell Khu, Jennifer Landau

Illustration Credits: Jamie Grecco
Photo Credits: p. 7 © David Lees/CORBIS; p. 8 © Peter A. Juley & Son Collection, Smithsonian American Art Museum; p. 9 © The Roland P. Murdock Collection, Wichita Art Museum, Wichita, Kansas; pp. 12, 14 © One Mile Up, Incorporated; pp. 16, 20 © Darrell Gulin/CORBIS; p. 18 © Buddy Mays/CORBIS; p. 22 © The Kansas State Historical Society; p. 24 © Philip Gould/CORBIS; p. 26 © Lowell Georgia/CORBIS; p. 28 © Joseph Sohm; ChromoSohm Inc./CORBIS.

Deinard, Jenny
     How to draw Kansas's sights and symbols / Jenny Deinard.
        p. cm. — (A kid's guide to drawing America)
     Includes index.
     Summary: This book explains how to draw some of Kansas's sights and symbols, including the state seal, the official flower, and the Hollenberg Station, an exchange station for the Pony Express.
     ISBN 0-8239-6072-2
     1. Emblems, State—Kansas—Juvenile literature 2. Kansas in art—Juvenile literature
3. Drawing—Technique—Juvenile literature   [1. Emblems, State—Kansas   2. Kansas
3. Drawing—Technique]   I. Title   II. Series
        2001
     743'.8'09781–dc21

Manufactured in the United States of America

CONTENTS

Let's Draw Kansas

The state of Kansas got its name from some Native American groups, including the Omaha and Dakota Sioux, that lived in the area. "Kansas" is the French way of spelling "KaNze," or "south wind," in their Native American language. Today the state has many industries, including aircraft manufacturing, construction, food processing, printing and publishing, and health care. Its farmland is host to cattle, wheat, corn, sorghum, soybeans, and hogs. In fact Kansas produces 20 billion pounds (9 billion kg) of wheat per year, much of it used to make bread and cereal. That is why the state is often called the Breadbasket of America. Kansas is also home to an animal called a pronghorn, an antelope-like animal that can run more than 60 miles an hour (97 km/h). Pronghorns are the fastest animals in North America.

You can learn about Kansas's sights and symbols as well as how to draw them with this book. Each drawing begins with a simple shape. You will add other shapes to this one. Directions under each drawing explain how to do the step. New steps are shown in red. The drawing terms show you some of the shapes and words used throughout this book. The last step of many drawings is to add shading.

You will need the following supplies to draw Kansas's sights and symbols:

- A sketch pad
- An eraser
- A number 2 pencil
- A pencil sharpener

These are some of the shapes and drawing terms you need to know to draw Kansas's sights and symbols:

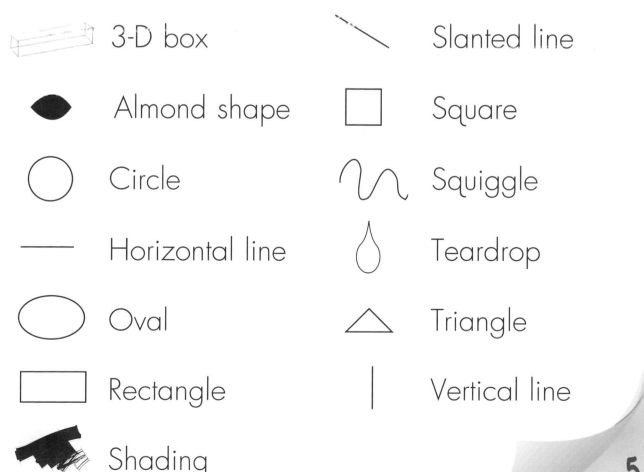

3-D box

Slanted line

Almond shape

Square

Circle

Squiggle

Horizontal line

Teardrop

Oval

Triangle

Rectangle

Vertical line

Shading

The Sunflower State

On January 29, 1861, Kansas became the thirty-fourth state to join the United States. Kansas is the fifteenth-largest state in the country and covers 82,282 square miles (213,109 sq km) of land. Kansas has a population of 2,654,100. The capital city of Kansas is Topeka. The most populated city is Wichita, with more than 300,000 residents.

Kansas's official nickname is the Sunflower State because acres of wild sunflowers grow on the state's plains. Kansas is also called the Squatter State because of the pioneers who traveled west and ended up living in the territory. Due to Kansas's dangerous weather, the state is also known as the Cyclone State. You might remember that Dorothy, from the movie *The Wizard of Oz*, was swept away by a tornado in Kansas. In 1970, the largest hailstone on record fell from the sky in Coffeyville, Kansas. It was 17½ inches (44 cm) wide and weighed nearly 2 pounds (.9 kg)!

The sunflower gets its name because its big, yellow flowers remind us of the sun.

Kansas Artist

John Steuart Curry

John Steuart Curry was born in 1897, on a farm near Dunavant, Kansas. Although he lived most of his life on the East Coast and in Wisconsin, he always considered himself a Kansas artist. His paintings were dramatic looking but realistic. John Curry's work became known as American regionalism because he painted a particular region in America. In the case of Curry's paintings, this region was the American Midwest. Between 1937 and 1942, Curry painted murals, or large wall paintings, on the walls of the statehouse in Topeka, Kansas. Curry's first mural, entitled *Tragic Prelude*, showed the abolitionist John Brown, who murdered five slave owners in Kansas in 1857. Many people from Kansas felt that Curry's murals were too violent and upsetting. They pointed out all of the mistakes that he had made in his work. Heartbroken, Curry left Kansas in 1941 and returned to Wisconsin, where he died in 1946. In 1997, the state of Kansas held a birthday celebration on what would have been Curry's one hundredth birthday. During the celebration, there was an official apology for the treatment of Curry over the statehouse murals, and recognition of the importance of his work, especially the murals that he painted for his boyhood state.

The Line Storm was painted in oil on canvas. A line storm is a harsh storm that sometimes occurs during the equinoxes, the two days of the year when day and night are equal in length all over the world. Like many of Curry's paintings, *The Line Storm* shows the drama and danger of rural life.

Map of Kansas

Map of the Continental United States

Kansas is rectangular in shape. Only its northeast corner has a jagged border, which is formed by the Missouri River. Kansas borders Nebraska, Missouri, Oklahoma, and Colorado. Mount Sunflower is the state's highest point. It measures 4,039 feet (1,231 m) above sea level. Near Elkart lie 23 miles (37 km) of the Santa Fe Trail's Cimarron Route, the longest section of the trail on public land. Emigrants used the Santa Fe Trail to travel west in the nineteenth century. People would load their belongings into covered wagons and travel hundreds of miles on this trail that went from Missouri to New Mexico. Kansas has one national preserve, the Tallgrass Prairie National Preserve.

1

Draw a rectangle.

2

Using the rectangle as a guide, draw the shape of Kansas.

3

Erase extra lines. Draw a triangle to mark the Mine Creek Battlefield.

4

Draw a square to mark Fort Hays.

5

Draw a triangle and rectangle to mark Cheney State Park.

6

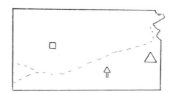

Draw a dotted line to mark where the Santa Fe Trail runs through Kansas.

7

Draw a star to mark Topeka, the state capital.

☆ Topeka
- - - Santa Fe Trail
☐ Fort Hays
⌂ Cheney State Park
△ Mine Creek Battlefield

8

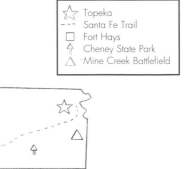

Erase extra lines in the star. Check the key to make sure you have added all of Kansas's highlights.

The State Seal

In 1861, John J. Ingalls designed Kansas's state seal. Ingalls was a lawyer and Kansas's state secretary. "Great Seal of the State of Kansas" and Kansas's statehood date are written around the seal's border. Kansas's motto, *Ad*

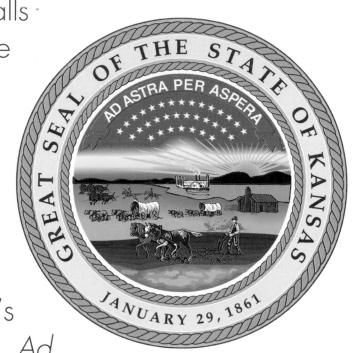

Astra Per Aspera, is written on the seal. It means, "to the stars through difficulties," in Latin. The motto refers to the pioneers who braved hard times in the years before Kansas became a state. The rising sun represents the East. Pioneers traveled from the East to Kansas hoping to find their fortune. The farmer working on his land with oxen reminds us of the importance of agriculture to the state. Behind the farmer is a herd of American buffalo, the state's official animal.

1

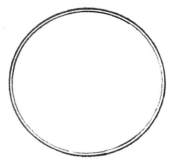

Draw two circles, one inside the other.

2

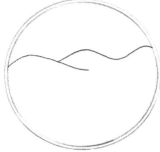

Draw wavy lines for mountains.

3

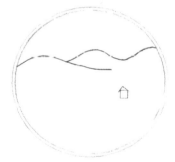

Add a square and a triangle for the farmer's cabin.

4

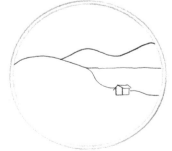

Add a square and rectangle to finish the cabin. Add two wavy lines to follow the shape of the water.

5

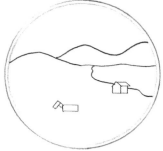

Draw three rectangles for the shape of the horse's body.

6

Add four small rectangles for the horse's legs, a triangle for its tail, and wavy lines to indicate the body. Erase extra lines.

7

Draw a circle for the man's head and rectangles for his body and arm. Add two parallel horizontal lines for a path.

8

Add a half circle for the sun. Add other detail as shown.

13

The State Flag

The state flag of Kansas was adopted in 1927. The flag measures 3 feet (91 cm) by 5 feet (152 cm). The state seal is centered on a dark blue background. There are 34 stars above the seal to show that Kansas was the thirty-fourth state to join the United States. On top of the stars is the official state motto, *Ad Astra Per Aspera*. The state's official flower, the sunflower, is above a gold-and-blue bar. Below the seal is the word "Kansas" in gold block letters. This was added to the flag in 1961.

1

Draw a large rectangle for the flag's background.

2

Draw an oval for the flower's center.

3

Draw about 20 short, straight lines around the oval for the center of each petal.

4

Using those short lines as guides, draw in the petals by using rounded V shapes.

5

Draw two triangles for the shape of the flower's leaves.

6

Erase any extra lines. Draw a thin rectangle with rounded edges

7

Draw five slanted lines inside the rectangle.

8

Erase any extra lines and smudges. Add the state seal under your rectangle. Add the word "KANSAS" at the bottom of your flag. Add detail to the thin rectangle.

The Wild Native Sunflower

The wild native sunflower became the Kansas state flower on March 13, 1903. However, the sunflower may not be native to the state. Sunflower seeds probably clung to the wagon wheels of travelers coming from southwestern states. Some people believe that the sunflower is native to the state because of sunflower images that were found on ancient urns in the nearby states of Missouri and Arkansas. Wherever the sunflower came from, today it is a big part of Kansas's culture. It is on the state flag and seal, and the Sunflower State is Kansas's official nickname.

1

Draw a circle for the center of the flower.

2

Draw a larger circle around the first circle.

3

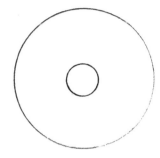

Draw about 20 lines from the first circle to the second. These lines will mark where each petal of the sunflower should go.

4

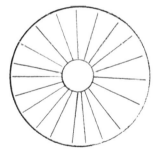

Erase the large circle.

5

Draw the tips of the petals using a V shape.

6

Draw lines from the end of each V to the center of the sunflower.

7

Erase any overlapping lines. Add shading and detail to your flower, and you're done.

The Cottonwood Tree

On March 23, 1937, Kansas adopted the cottonwood tree *(Populus deltoides Bartr)* as its state tree. The pioneers planted this kind of tree because it grew well in Kansas soil. The cottonwood is a large tree that can grow to 100 feet (30 m) tall and that has a trunk that can get up to 5 feet (1.5 m) in diameter. The tree got its name from the fluffy, white seeds that the trees produce in the summer.

Cottonwood trees often grow near rivers and streams. When pioneers crossed the plains and the prairies of Kansas, they traveled for a long time without seeing any trees. For the traveling pioneers, trees meant that both water and firewood were close at hand.

1

Draw a rectangle.

2

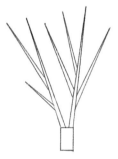

Draw two thin triangles above the rectangle for branches.

3

Draw five thin triangles to finish the branches.

4

Erase extra lines and round off the corners where your branches meet.

5

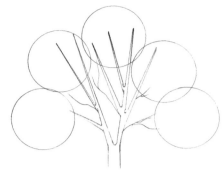

Add five circles around the tree to create the shape of the leaves. Add wavy lines for thin branches.

6

Using the circles as guides, start drawing in your leaves using squiggles.

7

Finish drawing in the leaves. Erase extra lines.

8

Add shading and detail to your tree. Erase any extra smudges, and you're done.

The Western Meadowlark

The western meadowlark (*Sturnella neglecta*) is Kansas's official state bird. There are both eastern and western meadowlarks in North America. Western meadowlarks prefer the drier, western areas of the United States. The two meadowlarks look very much alike. The western meadowlark has a yellow underbelly, and a back with black, brown, and white streaks. The birds develop a black *V* on their breast when they reach adulthood. They grow to a ½ inch (1.3 cm) long. The western meadowlark has a garbled singing voice. The eastern meadowlark has a simple, clear whistle. The female meadowlark of both species lays about five white eggs with reddish brown spots once or twice a year.

1

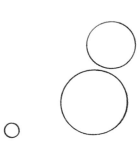

Draw three circles to begin the meadowlark's head and body.

2

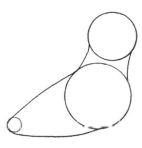

Connect the circles to form the bird's body.

3

Erase any extra lines. Add a small circle for the bird's eye.

4

Draw triangles for the bird's beak and for its wing.

5

Erase extra lines. Draw four slanted lines for the bird's legs.

6

Draw lines for the bird's feet and a triangle for its tail.

7

Erase extra lines. Add detail and shading. Use your finger to smudge the pencil lines.

The Lecompton Constitutional Hall

Lecompton was the capital of the Kansas territory from 1855 until 1861, the year Kansas became a state. In 1857, it was in this hall that the government made the controversial decision to take away land from Native Americans to make it available to white settlers. In the same year, delegates met at the Lecompton Constitutional Convention to write a document to make Kansas a state. There was disagreement about whether Kansas would become a pro- or antislavery state. At the time, the United States was dealing with this issue on a national level. The disagreement in Kansas drew so much attention that many historians believe that it helped to push the country into the Civil War.

1

Draw two triangles, one slightly smaller than the other.

2

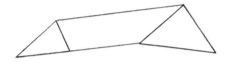

Connect the two triangles to form the roof.

3

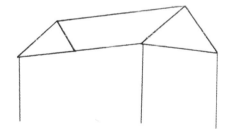

Add three straight lines.

4

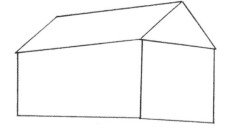

Connect the lines to form the outline of the Lecompton Constitutional Hall.
Erase extra lines.

5

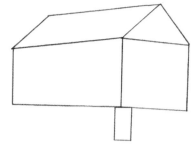

Add a small rectangle to begin drawing the podium.

6

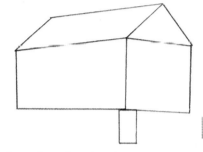

Add a short line for the far end of the podium.

7

Connect the short line to the rectangle. Draw rectangles for windows and doors.

8

Add shading and detail to the building. You can also add a flag and some trees.

The Hollenberg Station

The Hollenberg Station State Historic Site is located near Hanover, Kansas. Between 1860 and 1861, this is where Pony Express riders stopped to change for fresh ponies. Pony Express riders delivered mail across the country, from St. Joseph, Missouri, to Sacramento, California. The Hollenberg Station was a place where travelers bought supplies, had a meal, and rested for the night. The Hollenberg Station began as a one-room cabin and grew to a five-room building. The Hollenberg Station is the only Pony Express station that remains unchanged from its original form and that still stands exactly where it stood in the nineteenth century.

1

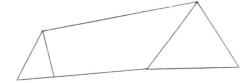

Start by drawing a large triangle and a smaller triangle.

2

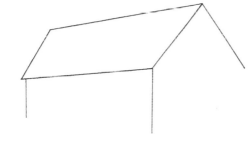

Then connect the two triangles to form the roof.

3

Add two straight lines. Erase extra lines.

4

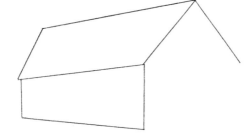

Connect the lines to form the side of the building.

5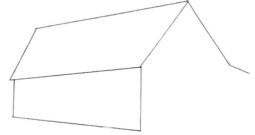

Add a short, slanted line from the right side of the roof.

6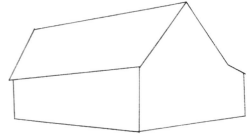

Add two straight lines to finish the shape of the building.

7

Use rectangles to add windows and a door.

8

Add shading and detail to the station, and you're done.

The American Buffalo

The American buffalo *(Bison americanus)* became Kansas's state animal on March 28, 1955. The American buffalo, also called the bison, was once the most common grazing animal in North America. In 1871, near Dodge City, Kansas, it was estimated that a single herd contained more than four million buffalo! Buffalo weigh about 1 ton (.9 t) and can run about 35 miles per hour (56 km/hr). Between 1860 and 1880, millions of American buffalo were killed by hunters. In the beginning of the twentieth century, only about 1,000 were left. Today the American buffalo are safe from extinction. They can be seen grazing in Kansas's prairies.

1

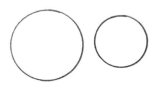

Draw two circles for the buffalo's body.

2

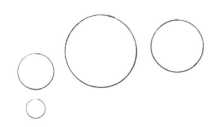

Add two more circles for the buffalo's head.

3

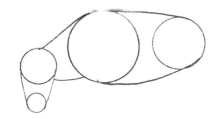

Connect the circles.

4

Erase extra lines.

5

Draw four triangles for the tops of the buffalo's legs.

6

Add four rectangles for the bottoms of the buffalo's legs.

7

Erase extra lines. Add the buffalo's horns, eyes, and tail.

8

To finish your buffalo, erase extra lines. Add detail and shading. You can use your finger to smudge the pencil lines.

27

Kansas's Capitol

The Kansas capitol building took more than 37 years to build. It was officially completed in March 1903. The building, which stands in the state's capital city of Topeka, is in the Italian Renaissance Revival style. It is one of the largest capitol buildings in the United States with more than 300,000 square feet (27,871 sq m). Much of the stone used in construction came from quarries in Topeka and Junction City, Kansas. The dome is 304 feet (93 m) tall, which is taller than the dome of the U.S. Capitol in Washington, D.C.! More than 20 acres (8 ha) of land surround the building as do many statues, including one of Abraham Lincoln, one of a pioneer woman and child, and a replica of the Statue of Liberty.

1

Draw two rectangles for the outline of the building.

2

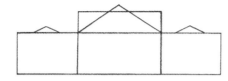

Add two small triangles and one large triangle.

3

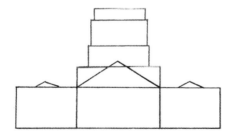

Draw three rectangles on top of the building to form the base of the dome.

4

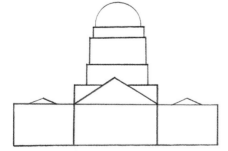

Add a half circle for the dome.

5

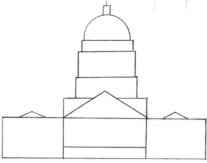

Add a rectangle and a short, straight line for the peak of the dome. Also draw a straight line across the front of the building.

6

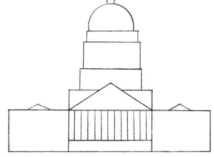

Add thin rectangles for the building's columns.

7

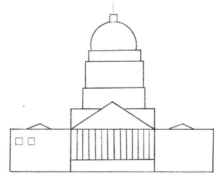

Draw in the windows with small squares.

8

Add shading and detail to your building. Erase any extra smudges, and you're done.

29

Kansas State Facts

Statehood	January 29, 1861, 34th state
Area	82,282 square miles (213,109 sq km)
Population	2,654,100
Capital	Topeka, population, 119,700
Most Populated City	Wichita, population, 320,400
Industries	Aircraft manufacturing, transportation equipment, construction, food processing
Agriculture	Cattle, wheat, corn, sorghum, soybeans
Animal	American buffalo
Tree	Cottonwood
Nickname	The Sunflower State
Motto	To the Stars Through Difficulties
Bird	Western meadowlark
Flower	Wild native sunflower
Reptile	Ornate box turtle
Insect	Honeybee
Amphibian	Barred tiger salamander
Soil	Harney
Song	"Home on the Range"
Marches	"The Kansas March" and "Here's Kansas"

Glossary

abolitionist (ah-buh-LIH-shun-ist) Someone who worked to end slavery.

adopted (uh-DOPT-ed) To have accepted or approved something.

agriculture (A-grih-kul-cher) Having to do with farms or farming.

Civil War (SIH-vul WOR) The war fought between the northern and southern states of America from 1861 to 1865.

controversial (kon-truh-VUR-shul) Causing an argument.

culture (KUL-chur) The beliefs, customs, art, and religions of a group of people.

cyclone (SY-klohn) A storm with very powerful winds.

delegates (DEH-lih-gets) People acting on behalf of another person or a group of people.

emigrants (EH-mih-grints) People who have left a country to settle somewhere else.

extinction (ik STINK-shun) When something no longer exists.

industries (IN-dus-treez) Systems of work, or labor.

preserve (prih-ZURV) An area set aside to protect plants and animals.

processing (PRAH-ses-ing) Treating or changing something using a special series of steps.

quarries (KWOR-eez) Areas of land where stones for building can be found.

Renaissance Revival style (REH-nuh-sahns ree-VY-vul STYL) A style of architecture that resembles Italian design between the fourteenth and seventeenth centuries.

replica (REH-plih-kuh) A copy.

represents (reh-prih-ZENTZ) Stands for.

sorghum (SOR-gum) Grasses that are like Indian corn.

Index

Web Sites

To find out more about Kansas, check out this Web site:
www.state.ks.us